This book did not hatch all by itself. The author wishes to thank the following ornithologists for their assistance in checking the manuscript for scientific accuracy, and for their helpful suggestions: Professor V. C. Wynne-Edwards, Chairman, Department of Zoology, Aberdeen University, Aberdeen, Scotland; Professor J. W. Stack, Director of The Museum, Michigan State College, East Lansing, Michigan; Dean Amadon, Ph.D., Associate Curator, Department of Birds, The American Museum of Natural History, New York City. Thanks also to Mrs. L. M. Terrill of the Redpath Library, McGill University, Montreal, and the librarians of the Detroit Public Library, Detroit, Michigan, for their generous assistance; and to Margaret Gossett, who also brooded.

FOURTH PRINTING

Printed in the U.S.A. by the Polygraphic Company of America
Published in Canada by Ambassador Books, Ltd., Toronto 1, Ont.

THE FIRST
BOOK OF
BIRDS

WRITTEN AND ILLUSTRATED BY

MARGARET WILLIAMSON

author and illustrator of THE FIRST BOOK OF BUGS

FW

FRANKLIN WATTS, INC.
699 Madison Avenue, New York 21, N.Y.

A BIRD IS ITSELF

A bird could never be mistaken for a dog or a lizard or a butterfly. A bird is simply a bird. Although there are many kinds of birds, they look and behave so much alike you can always tell them from other animals.

You might think a bird is different because it flies. But some birds—penguins and ostriches, for example—cannot fly at all. And some other animals can. Bats and insects do.

So, although flying is important to most birds, there are two more important things that really make a bird a bird.

First, all birds live in a hurry. Everything about a bird is busy and quick. Even when it stops to rest or sleep, it breathes faster than any other animal on earth. Also, its heart beats faster. Our own hearts beat about eighty times a minute. But a canary's heart beats one thousand times a minute. When you hold a bird in your hands, you can feel its heart pumping faster than you can count.

6

Birds are busy—   summer

A bird feels very warm, too. Its temperature is higher than that of any other creature in the world. If you had a temperature of 106 degrees, it would mean that you were very sick. But most birds feel bright and chirpy with temperatures of 106 degrees—and some have even higher temperatures.

With such quick breathing and such warm bodies and such strong hearts beating so quickly, it's no wonder birds are lively.

To keep the warmth of their bodies from going off into the air, birds have feathers. That is the second important way to tell a bird from any other animal. *All birds have feathers.* They are the only animals that do.

The color and shape of birds' feathers help us to tell one kind of bird from another. However, this book is about more than telling birds apart. It is about all the many things that make a bird a bird and all the fascinating ways birds have of living their own special kinds of lives.

ABOUT FEATHERS

Every bird has three main kinds of feathers: contour feathers that cover most of its body; an undercoat of soft, downy feathers; and a few hair-like feathers called "filoplumes."

7

and   winter

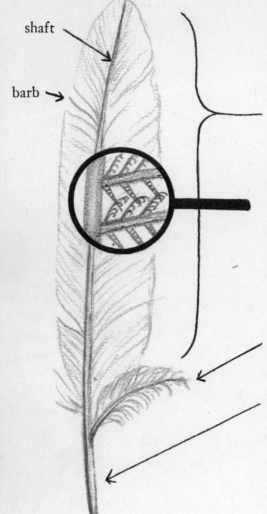

shaft

barb

CONTOUR FEATHER

CONTOUR FEATHER

SHAFT. Stiff and solid except for the hollow calamus, which fits into the bird's skin.

VANE. Looks like thin silky material lined with fine grooves. Really, it is made of two fringes of barbs, one growing out from each side of the shaft. Each barb branches into two rows of tiny branchlets. Hooks and notches on the branchlets fit together and lock each barb to its neighbors. It is as if the barbs were all zippered together to make a covering without holes.

AFTERSHAFT. A tiny duplicate of the main feather. Some birds don't have aftershafts.

CALAMUS. The hollow part of the shaft. The calamus fits into the bird's skin here.

The big contour feathers in a bird's wings are called flight feathers. Their barbs are especially well zippered together, making the feathers stiff and firm so that they act as a sail when they strike the air.

FLIGHT FEATHER

8

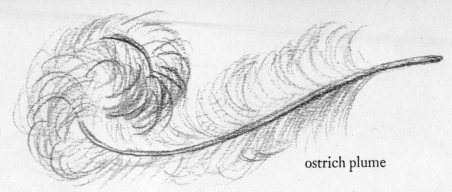

ostrich plume

Some birds have contour feathers called plumes, for "show." An ostrich plume is soft and fluffy. It has long barbs and branchlets which are not zippered together. An egret plume is long and filmy. It has a long shaft with unzipped barbs.

Beneath the contour feathers on most birds there is a warm undercoat of soft fluffy feathers called "down." These do not have long stiff shafts. The barbs branch from the calamus like hairs from a paintbrush, and there are no hooks or notches to zip the barbs together.

Water birds, like ducks and geese, have especially thick coats of down feathers. These are like warm underwear, protecting birds from the cold water. The first feathers that most birds have are also down feathers. They are like the soft fluff of baby chicks.

Besides down and contour feathers, there are the long, hair-like feathers called filoplumes. No one really knows what these are for.

There are also some short black prickles, particularly on the birds' wings. These are called "pinfeathers," but they aren't a different kind of feather. They are new feathers pushing out from the birds' skin. The black prickles are hard coverings which protect the delicate new feathers until they are strong. Then the coverings split and peel off, and the barbs of the feathers unfold.

filoplume

pinfeather

pinfeather unfolding

down feather

The golden-crowned king-
let breeds in Canada and
at high altitudes in the
United States. Its nest is
often in an evergreen tree.

↓

↑

The Eastern towhee loves
brushy places and is found
over the eastern part of
the United States and
southern Canada. It sings
its own name, "tow-hee."

↑

The cedar waxwing gets
part of its name from the
red tips on its wing feathers which look like drops
of red sealing wax. It loves
to eat cherries.

BIRDS TO LOOK FOR IN
over most of

The yellow warbler likes
open country with plenty
of trees and bushes nearby
where it can look for in-
sects on the leaves and
branches.

↓

The chickadee sings
"chick-a-dee-dee" as it
looks for seeds and insects
about trees. It is often seen
around our houses in
wintertime.

↓

↑

The rose-breasted gros-
beak is a summer resident
in woods and orchards of
eastern North America. In
fall, the male becomes
somewhat streaked, a little
like the female.

The redstart is easy to see darting through the green trees. The female is olive green where the male is black, and yellow where he is red.

↓

↑

The screech owl comes in two colors. It may be spotted or streaked in rusty red or grayish brown. It cries "Oo-oo-oo" at night, and sounds very sad.

↑

The junco, or "snowbird," visits our woods and backyards in winter. In summer, it prefers to live in Canada because it likes cool weather.

WOODSY OR BRUSHY PLACES
North America

The downy woodpecker is found in our woods and also about our dooryards, winter and summer. Only the male wears the bright red patch on his head.

↓

The brown creeper creeps spirally up a tree, looking for insects and their eggs and larvae. It is seen mostly in cold weather.

↓

↑

The white-breasted nuthatch often walks down a tree headfirst, looking for its dinner. It stays the year round, even in the cold snowy North.

preening

wiping bill

FINE FEATHERS MAKE FINE BIRDS

If you rub a contour feather up and down roughly the barbs separate and become tangled. The hooks have to be helped back into place. That is just what a bird does when it sits on a branch and combs its feathers with its beak after the wind has ruffled them. This is called "preening."

Most birds have a large oil gland at the base of their tails. They preen their feathers by combing the oil through them with their bills. Some scientists think that this keeps the feathers waterproof. That would explain why "water runs off a duck's back."

Birds are very fussy about keeping their feathers clean and tidy. Besides preening, some often take baths. They love to splash in the water, even in wintertime. They send splashes high in the air to make themselves a shower. Some birds prefer dry cleaning to a wet shampoo. They squirm and flutter in the dust. This probably helps keep them free of lice.

drinking

NEW FEATHERS FOR OLD

Feathers wear out just as clothes do. When they break and fray, the old feathers are pushed out by new ones that grow under them. This feather-changing is called molting. Most birds molt once a year, usually in late summer or early fall. Some kinds of birds take only a few weeks to do this. Other kinds take several months.

Among flying birds, two wing or tail feathers usually drop out at a time—one on either side of the bird. A second pair falls when the pair before it is almost grown in. In this way, birds keep enough feathers to fly about and catch their food and dodge their enemies. Penguins, though, lose their feathers in handfuls at a time. So do ducks and geese, and they have to hide until they can fly again. As they are swimming birds, they manage to catch food even though they have lost their flying feathers.

king penguin molting

Some kinds of birds molt twice: once in the fall and once in the spring. In spring, they do not usually lose their wing and tail feathers, but they grow new and brightly colored contour feathers.

bathing and shaking off

the male scarlet tanager molts twice a year

summer   winter

FEATHERS ARE PROTECTION

Some birds' feathers are colored so that they act as a camouflage in escaping from enemies. They may be spotted with patches of color that match the dead grass or earth or old leaves or sand or pebbles where the birds live. Birds who live where there are no trees or cliffs in which to hide from faster and stronger enemies are likely to have camouflage coloring. Females and young birds, who need the most protection, often match their hiding places more than males do.

When it rains, a bird's oiled and zippered feathers make a good raincoat. When it is cold, a bird fluffs out its feathers, holding a layer of warm air next to its skin. When it is hot, a bird can't take its feathers off, but it can flatten them into a very thin layer.

BIRDS ARE BUILT FOR FLYING

A bird's body is as streamlined as an airplane, so that it slips easily through the air. Even its feathers point smoothly back from head to tail. A bird has big strong breast muscles that work its wings, which are also streamlined.

Though it is very strong, a bird is lightly built. Its wings are made mostly of light feathers that overlap one another. There are only a few bones along the wings' front edges, and some of them are hollow and filled with air. So are many of the other bones in a bird's body. Besides, a bird has inside itself several sacs connected with its lungs. These are filled with air, like balloons. A bird is much lighter than it would be if all these air spaces were filled with muscle or fat.

14

birds are streamlined

Air sacs are useful in other ways. Birds can't perspire as people and animals do, so the fresh air in the air sacs cools them inside and keeps them from getting overheated when they fly very fast. Water birds use their air sacs as storehouses for air when they dive underwater. And flying birds cannot lose their breath because with each flap their strong flying muscles also help pump stale air out of their lungs and air sacs. The faster a bird flies, the faster its muscles work, the faster it pumps air, and the easier it breathes.

primary flight feathers

secondary flight feathers

wing coverts

only this much of wing is bone

wing can be folded neatly when bird rests

HOW BIRDS FLY

When a bird flies, it flaps its wings up and down. A flap is like a jump, using wings instead of legs to jump with, and air instead of ground to jump upon. Pushing down on the air with its wings lifts a bird up and keeps it in the air.

A long-legged bird has an advantage on the take-off. It just springs into the air and folds its legs up. There is then enough room beneath its wings for a downward flap. A short-legged bird has

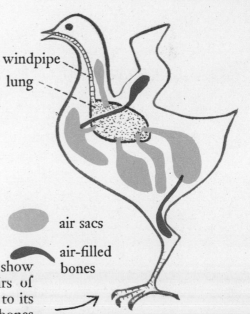

windpipe

lung

air sacs

air-filled bones

15

this diagram is just to show how a bird's five pairs of air sacs are connected to its lungs and air-filled bones

to spring higher into the air or dive down from a branch of a tree in order to give its wings room for the first flap. Most water birds have to paddle and kick along the water for quite a way before they take off. Some ducks shoot themselves into the air by a powerful sudden push with their wings against the water.

If you hold your hand outside a car window as you ride along, so that it is tilted up slightly in the direction you are going, the air will push your hand upward. As a bird flaps along, its wings are tilted in just the same way. The front edges of the wings are up and the feather edges behind are down. The air pushing up, and the tilt of the wings help to keep a bird in the air.

canvasbacks running
on water to take off

gannet plunging from
cliff to take off

Flapping its wings moves a bird forward. Both wings move up or down at the same time. At the start of a flap, the wings are up above the bird's back. On the downstroke, the wings move forward, then downward and backward. The wings push the air behind them. This shoves the bird ahead. On the upstroke, the wings move upward and backward to get ready for the next flap down. The faster a bird flaps, the faster it moves along.

To land, a bird twists its wings forward, with the underside facing front. They push against the air and act as a brake. A bird sometimes uses its tail as an extra brake by pushing it down and spreading it out fanwise.

To turn, a bird tilts its body and drags one wing in the direction it wants to go. Sometimes it steers using its tail as a rudder.

mallards landing

herring gulls gliding

Sometimes a bird glides, perhaps to rest its wings. As it glides, it drops lower and lower or goes slower and slower till finally it has to start flapping again to stay up in the air.

Some birds rise higher and higher in the sky on motionless, outstretched wings. This is called soaring. In the sky are warm, light air currents, rising through the heavier, colder air around them. To soar, birds let this warm rising air push against the underside of their wings and they travel up with it. Birds with big wings, like eagles and vultures, are the best soarers.

The shape of a bird's wings tells a lot about its habits. Swifts and swallows, who chase insects in the sky, have fairly long, pointed wings which are best in flying fast for a long time. They are also good for stopping and starting suddenly and for twisting and turning quickly.

Birds like ruffed grouse, that live in

steep bank
for fast turn

steering
with foot

twisting
tail to turn

hummingbirds

swift

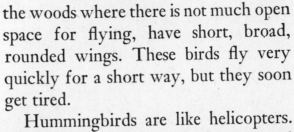

barn swallow

ruffed grouse

the woods where there is not much open space for flying, have short, broad, rounded wings. These birds fly very quickly for a short way, but they soon get tired.

Hummingbirds are like helicopters. With their tiny wings they buzz in and out and around flowers, sometimes hovering in one spot, sometimes flying backward instead of forward.

BIRDS REST, TOO

To keep in good condition for flying, birds have to rest. They sleep at night, for most of them cannot see well enough in the dark to move about. Owls are different. They see best at night, so they sleep by day.

Many birds sleep standing on their feet with their heads buried in the feather pillows of their shoulders, and their bills tucked into their wing feathers. Usually they find a hiding place where enemies can't find them.

bobwhites sleeping
(after R. B. Horsfall—courtesy National Audubon Society)

birds roosting

Ducks and swans often spend the night bobbing about on the water. A bobwhite and its family sleep together in a circle on the ground. Each one faces out, then if danger comes, the whole flock can scatter in many directions.

When the weather is cold some birds sleep in holes in the ground or in trees or in dead leaves. Some even snuggle under snowbanks.

Only a few birds, like owls and martins and pigeons, ever sleep in their nest, except when they are brooding eggs.

EYES AND EARS

Most birds are small creatures with few weapons to defend themselves. But they fly and move so quickly that most of them can outwit enemies many times their size.

To move quickly, a bird must be able to see well. A bird can use its eyes as a telescope one minute and as a microscope the next. Most birds have eyes on the sides of their heads so that they can see things on both sides at once, but not in front. When they look at anything close up and straight in front of them, they have to cock their heads to one side.

Owls, who prey on smaller birds and animals, have eyes in the front of their heads. They can't move their eyeballs so, to watch something moving, they "fix" their eyes on it and twist their necks.

20

an owl sees the same thing with both eyes— just as we do

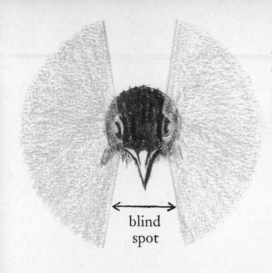

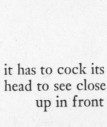

a bird with eyes on the sides of its head sees different things with each eye

blind spot

it has to cock its head to see close up in front

A bird has three eyelids. Two are much like ours, but the third one is transparent, and it moves across from side to side when a bird winks. That third eyelid wipes dust specks off, much as a windshield wiper does on a car. Scientists think it may also be drawn across the eye when a bird is flying, as protection against the wind.

A bird's ears are as keen as its eyes. Birds' ears are round holes opening on either side of their heads and surrounded by arrangements of feathers which help catch sound waves and steer them into the ears.

BIRDS HAVE DIFFERENCES

Though all birds have feathers, and though most of them are built for flying, still, birds are all shapes and sizes. They have a great variety of wings and feet and beaks, and all colors of feathers. For each kind of bird is fitted to live its own kind of life in the place it likes to live best.

Birds live in all sorts of places, so no two kinds of birds look exactly alike, though they all have the same parts.

the third eyelid being drawn across

hen's ear

osprey

belted
kingfisher

BIRDS TO LOOK FOR

The osprey, or "fish hawk," is found over rivers and
lakes through most of North America. It dives, feet
foremost, for the fish it likes to eat.

The belted kingfisher can be found along lakes and
rivers, ponds and streams, throughout North America. The male does not have the extra chestnut band
across his breast.

The red-winged blackbird usually builds its nest in
the reeds of a marsh or swamp. The female is a
dusty brown with a striped breast. It is found over
most of North America.

The green heron may be found almost anywhere
there is water in North America.

red-winged
blackbird

green heron

herring gull

bald eagle

ON, OR NEAR, WATER

The herring gull is the most common gull of our lakes and rivers and ocean shores.

The bald eagle, the national bird of the United States, stays close to lakes, rivers and ocean shores looking for dead fish to eat.

The Canada goose is the "honking" goose. It migrates in flocks, in V-shaped formations, in the fall.

The American merganser is a duck with a saw-toothed bill for catching slippery fish. The male has a greenish-black head and looks quite different from the female.

The spotted sandpiper lives along ocean beaches and lake shores and is the best-known sandpiper in North America. It teeters when standing still.

American merganser

Canada goose

spotted sandpiper

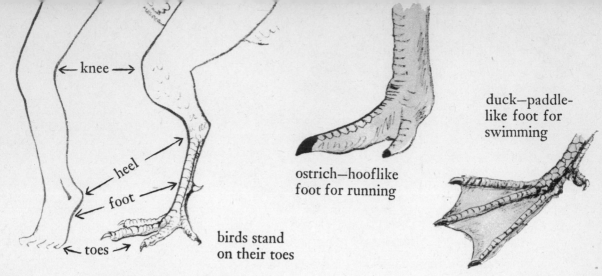

knee

heel

foot

toes

birds stand
on their toes

ostrich—hooflike
foot for running

duck—paddle-
like foot for
swimming

KINDS OF FEET

All birds have two feet.

Most birds use their feet to walk or hop or run. Others swim or climb or perch, too. Each bird has feet shaped best for the job they have to do.

Almost all birds have four toes on each foot. While they may look delicate, they are really very strong. They are long and wiry, and spread out. This gives them a good grip, and helps the bird to spring into the air suddenly, too.

The bones in a bird's legs are much like ours, but they are stretched out. What some people think is a bird's leg is really its anklebone, and what they think is its knee bent backward is really its heel. This springy kind of foot makes spraining an ankle impossible, and helps a bird land in a hurry and balance safely.

Swimming birds like ducks and geese have webbed feet which they use as paddles.

Birds like sparrows and starlings and warblers, that spend much time in trees, have feet each with three toes in front

cord and
toes loose

cord and
toes stretched tight

many perching birds'
legs work this way

24

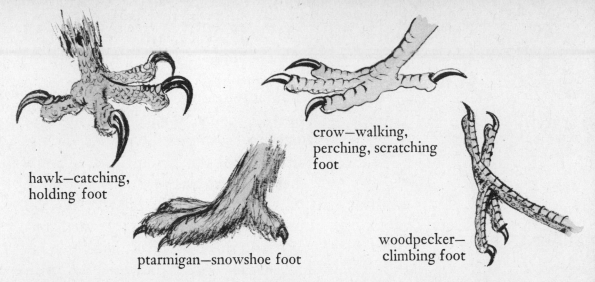

hawk—catching, holding foot

crow—walking, perching, scratching foot

ptarmigan—snowshoe foot

woodpecker—climbing foot

and one long one behind, for perching on branches. These birds can sleep perched on a twig without any danger of falling off. Each toe is connected with a cord that passes up inside its leg and over a kind of pulley at the joints. When the bird stands up, the cords are loose and its toes are free. When it bends its legs, the cords stretch tight and its toes curl around the branch.

Parrots and woodpeckers, that climb trees, have four toes all the same size, two in front and two behind on each foot. Their toes end in sharp claws that dig into the rough bark of tree trunks.

Ostriches cannot fly away from their enemies, but they can run as fast as horses. They have just two big, thick toes on each foot. Their feet are almost like hoofs.

WHAT BIRDS EAT

Birds, like other animals, eat food as fuel to keep their living engines going. Birds need a great deal of food. They spend much of their lives looking for things to eat.

Many birds are vegetarians. They eat only fruit and seeds or leaves or buds.

25

barn owl with mouse

Other birds are meat-eaters. Great horned owls eat small birds and small animals like mice and rabbits. Swifts and swallows eat flying insects. Some other birds eat beetles and ants or juicy grubs and worms. Most hawks prey on small birds, reptiles, and other small animals. And there are birds, like penguins and pelicans and cormorants, who fish for a living.

Some birds eat both meat and vegetables. Still others have changed their habits since they have been living near people. They eat left-over scraps and garbage. Sea gulls will even follow a ship for many miles just to live on the rubbish thrown overboard from a ship's galley.

HOW BIRDS CATCH FOOD

Birds have no teeth. They eat their food whole, or in large pieces. Instead of teeth, a bird has a hard, horny beak. Its shape helps the bird catch and eat the kind of food it likes. Beaks do the work of many tools.

hummingbird
sucking nectar

crows eating corn   26

nutcracker
bill of finch

knife and fork
bill of hawk

wrench bill
of crossbill

sieve bill of merganser

spear bill of heron

Birds like finches, who eat seeds and berries, have short, thick, pointed beaks that make good nutcrackers. A crossbill eats seeds, too, but from pine cones, and it has to twist the cone scales off to get them. Its bill is shaped to make a good crowbar or wrench.

A hummingbird uses its long, pointed beak as a probe to go deep inside flowers. It uses its long, tubular tongue as a straw to suck up the nectar.

Some woodpeckers use their long, pointed bills as chisels to get at the grubs which bore into trees. They have long, rough, sticky tongues to reach way into a grub's tunnel and rake it out.

Swifts and whippoorwills have tiny beaks but huge, gaping mouths which they keep wide open like bags, as they dash around the sky, catching insects.

Many ducks have broad, flat bills with fringed edges. They make good sieves. Their tongues are fringed, too. These ducks strain small animals and plants out of the mud and water as they swim along or as they tip or dive underwater to get food.

starlings
eating
garbage

cowbirds
catching flies

a brown pelican dives for its fish

Hawks and falcons and eagles have sharp, hooked bills. They use them as knives and forks to tear their prey to pieces after they have caught and held it in their long, strong claws.

Herons wade out in shallow water on their long legs. They have long, pointed bills that they use as spears to stab the fish that swim by, or the frogs that jump too near.

A kingfisher perches on a lookout bough over a stream. At the sight of a fish, it plunges into the water and comes up with the fish held crosswise in its bill. Then it tosses the fish into the air and swallows it head first.

Pelicans have long bills with huge, elastic pouches in their bottom halves. A brown pelican uses its pouch as a dip net to capture fish when it dives into the sea. The great white pelican uses the pouch to scoop up fish as it swims along the surface of the water.

Penguins and cormorants chase fish by swimming after them underwater. Penguins "fly" underwater, using their wings as paddles. Cormorants swim by using their wings and webbed feet.

a penguin "flies" underwater, chasing fish

(after L. R. Brightwell)

food pipe—"gullet"

crop

first part stomach

gizzard

vent

intestine

EATING WITHOUT CHEWING

Even though birds bolt their food without chewing it, they probably don't feel uncomfortable. They have their own way of taking care of food.

When a bird swallows, the food passes down a long, elastic tube called a "gullet," which is inside the bird's neck. The bottom of the gullet is often widened into a bag called a "crop." The food may stay there for hours to be softened or stored.

When it is ready, it passes into the bird's stomach. One part of the stomach pours juices over it, for digesting it. The other part is the gizzard, which is lined with tough skin, and has strong wall muscles for grinding the food to pieces.

A bird that eats hard seeds and grain always swallows small pebbles or pieces of shell, too. As the muscles force the inside walls of the gizzard together, the pebbles rub against the grain and grind it up. Of course, the pebbles and pieces of shell rub against each other, too, and gradually wear down so small that the bird gets rid of them along with the waste material from its food. That is why the bird has to swallow more pebbles every day or two.

Birds like owls and kingfishers, that eat their prey whole, cough up little balls of bones and skin and fur or scales when their meal is over. These are called pellets and they tell naturalists what the birds had for their last meal.

29

pellet of a barn owl
showing skull, fur,
bones of mice
(life size)

BIRDS START LIFE KNOWING HOW

Even though birds have a big brain for their size, and sharp eyes and ears to help them, they cannot figure things out by themselves as people do. A bird works mostly by instinct. That means it is born knowing how to do things it has never done before. It knows how to build its first nest and how to fly and how to sing, though sometimes it does better after it practices a bit. A bird has an instinct for almost everything it does.

BIRD LANGUAGE

Not all birds can sing songs, but almost all birds are able to tell things to one another. Most bird language is made up of simple signals for special occasions, just as we say "Hello" to greet someone, or "Oh" in surprise. A factory whistle means "Hurry up," and a motor horn means "Look out." Bird calls are like them, for they are short and clear and loud. They are meant to be heard, and often have to be acted upon quickly. Sometimes birds repeat them over and over again.

Some of the bird calls we know best are the "caw" of the crow, the "quack" of the duck, and the "coo" of the pigeon.

Mother birds have a special language for their young. A mother hen has a call to warn her chicks of danger, and to get them to follow her. She has another special clucking sound to coax the chicks to cuddle under her wings when it rains.

Young birds, too, have special peeps to catch their mother's attention if they want food or if they lose sight of her.

30

quack
quack

honk

Grown-up birds recognize their mates by their voices, just as we do our friends and family, without having to see them.

When birds fly together in flocks, they have "travel talk" for calling to one another. Geese honk back and forth when they are flying south. Starlings also have "let's come together" signals. They can be very noisy, finding one another and getting settled for the night.

Some birds are more talkative than others. A few birds never say anything at all. Storks don't, but they make a noise by clattering their beaks together when they meet.

Many perching birds, like robins and orioles and warblers, can sing songs as well as make noises and calls. They sing mostly in the spring.

Usually male birds, or cocks, do most of the singing. Females have only soft little notes to talk to their mates.

Most birds sing the same song every time, but the mockingbird is continually making up new ones. He is a mimic.

the brown thrasher sits on a high perch and sings most everything twice over

Killdee Kill-dee

the killdeer calls its own name

the eastern meadowlark has a clear whistle for a song

creakee

creakee

terns screaming at one another

He can imitate the quack of a duck or the pop of a cork or the squeak of a wheelbarrow or countless other things. Then he can take any of these sounds and make them into music. He can give the alarm call of a hen and fool the chicks, who scuttle beneath their mother for safety. Besides that, he has a fine song of his own which he sings by the hour in the moonlight.

Some of our finest wild bird musicians are the thrushes. Their notes are fine and high, and their songs are beautiful.

Birds have a music box called a "syrinx" at the bottom of their windpipes. The music box has several elastic membranes that are stretched or loosened by muscles. The membranes vibrate and make sounds when the air rushes past. A bird does not shape the sounds with its mouth, but with the muscles in its music box. Birds that have real songs have more complicated music boxes with more muscles than birds that have only calls.

A few birds have quite different ways of making noises. An emu has big pouches like balloons in its neck. It fills them with air, then empties them, to make a big noise. A woodpecker drums with its beak on a tin roof or drainpipe or dry limb.

The mockingbird can give the alarm call of a hen

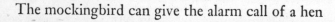

(after L. R. Brightwell)

hermit thrush

BIRDS IN SPRING

Springtime is birdtime in North America. Many birds go south for the winter. Then, as the days grow longer and warmer, they return by thousands.

The males usually come first. Now they have their brightest feathers and are singing their most beautiful songs. Each finds a likely spot for building a nest—safe as possible from the weather and from enemies, and with enough land around it so that there will be food for a family. This land becomes that bird's own "territory." It may be big—an eagle's is a few square miles in area. Or it may be only a few inches around the nest, like that of sea birds that nest close together in colonies and fish in the sea.

Each male shoos away any other male that trespasses on his property. They may just fluff out their feathers and rush at one another, flapping their wings, or they may fight with spurs on their legs or with their beaks. Most of the time a male songbird sits in some favorite spot in his territory and sings at the top of his lungs, warning everyone to stay away.

We know, of course, that birds don't think or plan or have feelings the way people do. A male bird just has instincts that guide him in these strange performances when he seems to be acting like a human being.

His loud singing attracts any female that is looking for a mate. When a female, or hen, drops down from the sky into his territory, the male bird puts on quite a performance for her. He "shows himself off," trying to win her as his mate.

33

FIGHTING AND

Blue jays know that owls are their enemies. Finding one in the daytime, they tease it unmercifully and may even drive it away. The owl never fights back till night comes.

A killdeer plays "hurt bird" to lure an enemy away from its nest. It limps along, dragging its wings and screaming loudly.

Many eggs and baby birds match their surroundings so closely that they are hidden from enemy eyes.

This duck hawk is trying to scare its rival away by looking as big and fierce as it can.

FOOLING ENEMIES

Many birds try to dodge their enemies.

Cocks fight each other with the spurs on their legs, pecking with their beaks and flapping their wings. (after L. R. Brightwell)

A frightened bittern "freezes," with its bill pointed to the sky, so that it looks like part of the reeds in the marshy places where it lives.

a female tern begs for a fish

(after Roland Green)

Besides singing, a male bird that is showing off in front of a female may either twitter or coo or crow, all the while fluttering his wings and posing or strutting about with fluffed-up feathers. He may skip or jump or turn or bow to the ground in front of her. He may even chase her, or he may put on flying exhibitions in the air above her. He does all kinds of things that show off his brightest feathers or any special ornaments he may have—for cocks are often much more brilliantly colored than hens.

Turkeys and peacocks spread their tail feathers, pigeons puff out their chests, umbrella and frigate birds blow up the big red pouches beneath their beaks. Parrots and ostriches collect bright things and present them to their hoped-for mates.

The hens usually act as if they did not notice all this. They may just turn their backs and go on eating. If a male has pleased a hen,

"ruff"

male birds may
wear special
ornaments

← caruncle

plumes

hummingbird

bell bird

wattle

turkey

penguins courting

a rooster struts and crows

though, she will finally go off with him as his mate. If not, the cock bird will try his luck elsewhere.

Among some birds, the males and females look very much alike. Then they usually show off to each other. Cranes bow and dance and skip and hop together. Terns pass a fish back and forth to one another. Great crested grebes come face to face, and shake their heads back and forth. Sometimes they separate and dive, coming up with bits of waterweed in their beaks, to offer to one another.

Most birds stay with their mates for a month or six weeks while they are bringing up their young. Then they may find new mates for the next brood. Others may stay together to raise the two or three broods often hatched in one summer.

Many birds, especially those that don't go south for the winter, pair for life.

a herring gull presents his mate with a sea shell

37

IN THE SPRINGTIME

An excited cormorant may do a back bend.

Cranes dance together. They hop and bow and skip. (after L.R. Brightwell)

The male marsh hawk puts on flying exhibitions for an admiring female.

At dawn, male prairie chickens hold tournaments. They blow up their orange neck sacs, make loud booming noises, and fight one another.

BIRDS ARE SHOW-OFFS

The male man-of-war bird blows up the big red pouch in his neck to impress the females.

A cormorant opens its mouth wide to show off the bright yellow lining inside.

The turkey gobbler fluffs up his feathers, spreads his tail, swells his head ornaments, rattles his wing quills, struts and gobbles to attract attention.

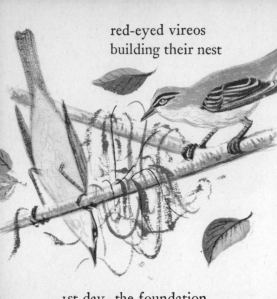

red-eyed vireos
building their nest

1st day—the foundation

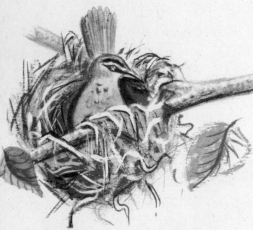

2nd, 3rd days—shaping it

4th day—
adding the
lining—finished

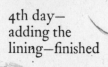

7th to 11th day
four eggs laid

BUILDING NESTS

As soon as two birds have paired off, they start to build their nest. Each kind of bird has its own kind of nest, and each kind of nest is in its own special spot. A bird knows by instinct just how and where to build its nest.

Robins mate and start building their nests as early as April, but May and June are the biggest nest-building months. It takes some birds about two weeks to collect their material and build their nests. Others, who work without stopping till they are finished, may take only a few days. Usually the female bird does the building, but sometimes the male bird gathers nesting materials and brings them to her. Other times he just sings.

There are all kinds of nests made in all kinds of ways. One of the simplest nests is just a scrape in the ground. It may or may not be lined with pebbles. A killdeer lays its eggs in this kind of nest.

robin's nest

A kingfisher burrows a long tunnel in a river bank and makes a room at the back where it lays its eggs. A screech owl saves itself trouble by finding an old hole in a tree trunk. A woodpecker often hacks its own hole in a dead tree. Some of the chips make a bed for the eggs, and the opening is just big enough for the birds to get through.

Many other birds build their nests of grasses or lichens or twigs or mud. The nests may be built on the ground, where they are usually well hidden, or they may be up in bushes or in trees or in barns or about houses, where they are harder to reach.

A song sparrow, like many other birds, often builds her cup-shaped nest of dead grasses, hidden beneath a clump of grass in a field.

41

song sparrow's nest

eagle's nest

Baltimore orioles

A Baltimore oriole weaves a swinging cradle of long grasses, plant fibers, hair, and strings, hanging from the twigs of a tree. While the oriole builds, she may work outside, clinging upside down, or most often, inside, pushing and pulling and stitching.

Father and mother barn swallow work together on the nest they build on rafters in a barn. It is made of mouthfuls of mud, stuck together and strengthened with straws. Often it is lined with chicken feathers and grass.

Most birds build a new nest every year. Some even build two or three a summer, one for each family they raise. Others repair their old ones and use them over again for a second brood. Eagles use the same nest year after year. Sometimes it may weigh over a ton.

42

red-headed
woodpecker

barn swallows

Some sea birds, like the murres, don't bother to make any nest. They lay their eggs high up on a narrow, rocky shelf, where they are well out of reach of intruders.

BIRDS' EGGS

Young birds hatch from eggs that are laid by the mother bird in her nest.

All female birds lay eggs, usually during the spring and summer. Eggs inside a bird's body start out looking like a bunch of yellow grapes. Each "grape" is the beginning of an egg. It is a tiny cell surrounded by yellow yolk. When one of these "grapes" swells to a certain size, it breaks away from the others and enters the funnel-shaped end of a long tube. The other end of the tube opens on the outside, beneath the bird's tail.

killdeer

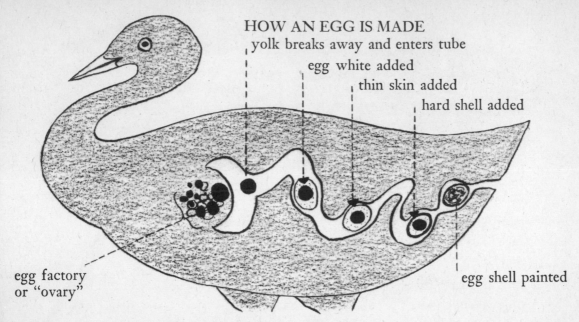

HOW AN EGG IS MADE

yolk breaks away and enters tube

egg white added

thin skin added

hard shell added

egg factory
or "ovary"

egg shell painted

The tube is more than just a passageway to the outside. It helps build the egg. First, the tube walls ooze out egg white, which is wrapped around the slowly revolving yolk. A little farther down the tube, material for the thin skin that goes on top of the white is squeezed on. After that, the walls pour a chalky substance around it. This hardens into the eggshell. And, last of all, the egg is painted by a liquid that comes from the tube walls—different colors for different birds. When the egg reaches the end of the tube, it is ready to be laid.

Birds' eggs are all sizes and shapes and colors. Bigger birds usually have bigger eggs. An ostrich egg is the largest. It will hold about eighteen hen's eggs. A hummingbird's egg is the tiniest— only as big as a bean.

Many eggs are oval-shaped like a hen's. But there are many other shapes, too. Owls lay eggs almost as round as golf balls. Murres lay pear-shaped eggs, which can't roll off their rocky ledges. Try rolling a pear, to see for yourself how it rolls in a circle.

an egg
may be

round

or

oval

or  pear-
shaped

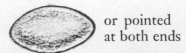 or pointed
at both ends

44

Some eggs are white. Most eggs are colors that match the ground and sky and leaves best—light tones of brown or blue or green or gray. They may be one plain color or they may be spotted or speckled or streaked.

An eggshell is not as solid as it looks and feels, but is dotted with very tiny air holes. Most of the air holes are at one end of the egg. They open into an air space between the shell and the skin. This is a storehouse of air for the baby bird. You can see this air space easily when you break open a hard-boiled egg.

The egg yolk is a storehouse of food for the growing bird inside the egg. The egg white acts as a watery cushion for the chick to lie in, as protection from bumps. It stores extra food, too. A tiny clear speck on top of the yolk is the part that grows into a baby bird. It is there only if the male and female birds have mated.

Not all eggs will grow into baby birds. Any egg without that tiny living clear speck will always be just an egg. Even an egg with a speck inside will not grow into a baby bird by itself. It must be kept warm.

hen's egg

hummingbird's egg

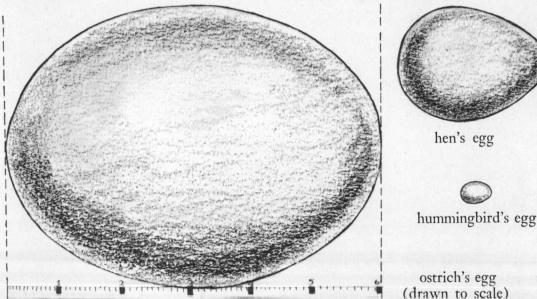

ostrich's egg
(drawn to scale)

mother robin brooding

BROODING AND HATCHING

The female bird is most often the one that sits on the eggs, or broods them, keeping them warm, particularly if the male is brightly colored and likely to attract the attention of enemies. He may help his mate, though, by feeding her while she sits. Sometimes the father and mother take turns sitting on the nest, and they find their own food when they are off duty.

Many birds have little ceremonies when it is time to change places on the nest. Gannets rub their heads together. Wandering albatrosses spread their wings out in greeting. Penguins bow low before one another with great dignity.

While the eggs are being brooded, the baby bird inside each one grows bigger and bigger every day. The yolk and the white grow smaller and smaller as the chick uses them up, till at last they are all gone and the baby bird fills the shell. It is curled up inside with its head bent over against its breast—almost like a sleeping bird.

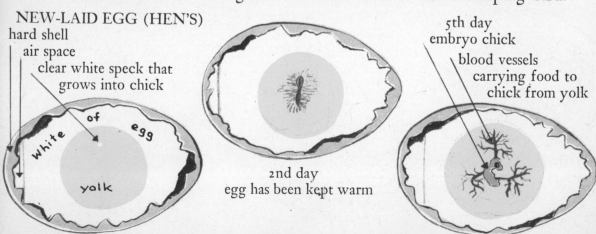

NEW-LAID EGG (HEN'S)
hard shell
air space
clear white speck that grows into chick
white of egg
yolk

2nd day
egg has been kept warm

5th day
embryo chick
blood vessels carrying food to chick from yolk

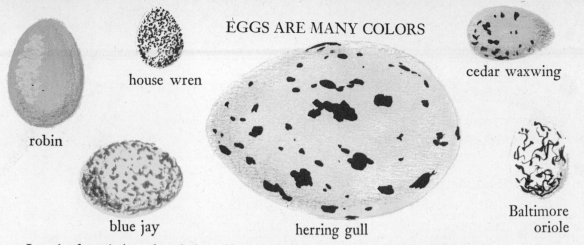

robin

house wren

cedar waxwing

blue jay

herring gull

Baltimore oriole

Just before it hatches it knocks its beak against the shell. The horny bump on the tip of its beak, called an "egg tooth," scratches and scrapes as the bird struggles to get out. First it chips one hole in the shell, then another and another and another, till the shell cracks right across and the baby bird wiggles out, all wet and tired. Afterward, the egg tooth falls off.

Usually, the bigger the bird the longer its egg takes to hatch. A huge emu's egg takes nine weeks to hatch, but a hummingbird's takes only ten days.

After the chicks have hatched, the mother usually drops the broken shells far away from the nest. Then there are no telltale signs to give away the secret of where her nest and young are hidden.

21st day

chick pecking to get out

19th day almost all yolk gone—feathers have grown

6 hours later

11th day white of egg almost gone

a baby pelican "fishes" for its dinner

YOUNG BIRDS

Some eggs have more yolk than others, so the chicks inside have more food and can stay inside the egg longer. When they hatch, their eyes are open and they have a downy fuzz all over their bodies. After drying off, they can run about and find food for themselves. Their mother only guides and protects them. The young of many ground-nesting birds are like this.

Most of the tree-nesting birds lay tiny eggs with little yolk. Their young are naked and blind when they hatch. They can't walk or fly or find food, and their parents must do everything for them.

Newly hatched birds must have lots of food. This is when the parents of helpless nestlings have the busiest time of their lives. A meal doesn't keep a tiny bird happy for long. The parent birds must make many trips, from dawn to sunset, to find enough food for their young.

A naturalist once watched two starlings bring sixteen thousand insects to their six children in one season. Another saw a young robin eat fourteen feet of earthworms in a day. And the parent birds had to search for each insect and each worm!

Parent birds have different ways of feeding their young. Perching birds just touch the bill of a young bird, and its

baby killdeer can feed themselves

mouth opens wide. Usually it is chirping loudly anyway, with its mouth open. The mouths of nestlings are brightly colored, often orange or yellow, and they may have bright red and blue spots which guide their parents to the right place to drop food.

A nestling is so helpless it can't even take the grubs or insects from the parents. They have to ram the food down its throat, and if the baby bird doesn't swallow as quick as a wink, they will pull the food out and plop it into another open mouth.

Wrens batter large caterpillars on a branch to soften them before feeding them to their young. Swallows snip off the wings of flies, and the water rail plucks off a spider's legs, making it easier for the young birds to swallow.

When a bird's food is hard to digest, the parent often partly digests it in its own crop or stomach before feeding it to its young. For the first few days, a parent pigeon takes a baby pigeon's bill in its mouth and pumps into it a creamy liquid called "pigeon's milk," made in the walls of the parent's crop. Later, young pigeons are fed partly digested food from the parents' crops until they can find food for themselves.

A pelican opens its enormous bill and the young poke their heads down to help themselves to the half-digested fish brought up from its stomach.

Fish-eating birds encourage their children to fish for themselves. The parents catch fish while the little ones watch. Then they drop the fish nearby in the water. Though the fish are dead, the young ones still have to pick them up in their beaks before they can eat. Swallows are said to do much the same thing, dropping insects from a distance as they swoop past, for their young to catch.

2 days old—
eyes closed,
no feathers

10 days
eyes open,
feathers
grown.
Two
birds
have
fallen
out and
died

GROWING UP

Birds that are helpless when they hatch stay in the nest until their feathers have grown big enough to use for flying. This usually takes at least a week or two. Most birds that are hatched naked stay in their nests for two or three weeks --and young albatrosses may be a year old before they can fly out to sea.

All young birds grow "first flying feathers." They are the same shape as their grown-up feathers, but often duller in color, or speckled for camouflage. As soon as the young birds have their first flying feathers, the old birds are anxious to get them out of the nest. They never push them out, but they do coax them. And sometimes young birds sneak out when the parents are away.

All birds have the instinct to fly, but the parent birds sometimes have to encourage them to make their first flight. The older birds may hold a piece of food to make the baby stretch its neck

exercising
wings

2 weeks old

first flight

blue jay

coot

gannet

duck

bittern

BABY BIRDS
(not drawn to scale)

so far beyond the nest that it topples over onto a branch. From there it will jump, fluttering its wings as it falls, while the old birds fly about, calling encouragement. But young birds need lots of experience before they can fly well, and during that time their parents still help to feed and protect them.

Water birds are encouraged to take to the water just as perching birds are encouraged to fly. A grebe will swim around with her young on her back. When she has to dive for food, the fledglings are dunked at the same time. In that way they get the feel of diving.

As soon as young birds can look after themselves, they leave the nest for good. A nest is a cradle, not a bed or a house. A little later their parents leave them to themselves, and then they are really on their own.

grebe
with young

safe landing

BIRDS IN WINTERTIME

Over northern countries, the four seasons are all different, and people and animals and plants change their habits with the seasons.

In late summer or fall, after the parent birds have raised their young, they molt their feathers. Then many of them fly south to their winter homes, along with the young birds. There they all eat and sleep and wander about a bit. They don't mate or build nests or lay eggs. When spring comes they return north. Other birds, like chickadees and juncos and some jays and starlings, stay north all winter.

Bird traveling to and from winter and summer homes is called "migration." Birds usually travel by the same air highways that their parents and great-great-grandparents did. We have learned a great deal about birds' amazing travels since someone first thought of fastening a small aluminum band around a bird's leg. Each band has a number and an address stamped on it. If the bird is captured or found dead, the band is returned to that address. There the record of that number is looked up, and scientists learn where and when the band was put on the bird's leg. By the records kept of bird-banding we have discovered where birds go in wintertime and what air highways they take.

But some things not even bird-banding can tell us. What makes birds migrate in the first place? How do they know the way? Why do they go to the same winter or summer homes each year?

They couldn't have decided to go south to escape the cold and lack of food. Many of them leave their nesting sites before the cold comes. They often return in the spring after the snow has melted and gone. So they don't know what winter is like.

52

banded
herring gull

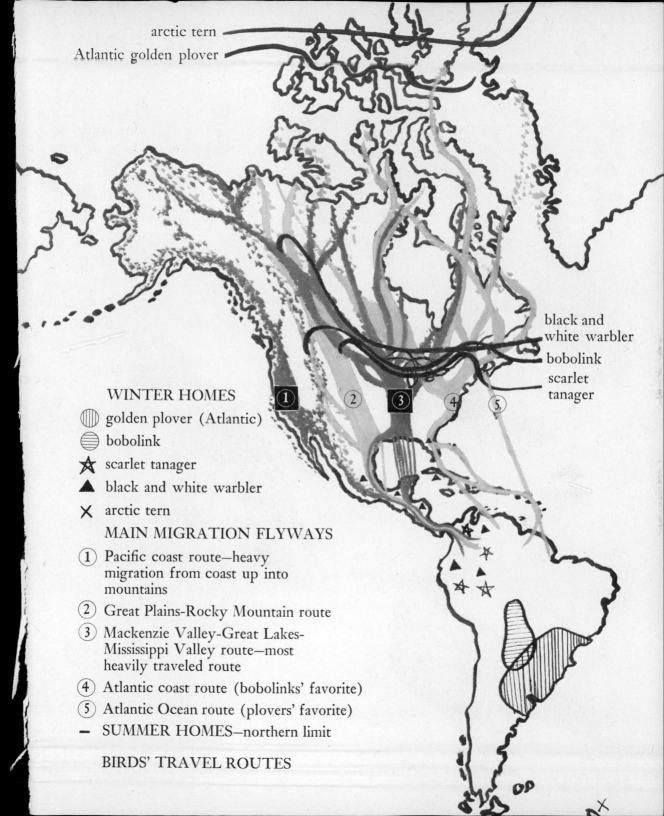

arctic tern
Atlantic golden plover

black and
white warbler
bobolink
scarlet
tanager

WINTER HOMES
golden plover (Atlantic)
bobolink
scarlet tanager
black and white warbler
arctic tern

MAIN MIGRATION FLYWAYS
① Pacific coast route—heavy
migration from coast up into
mountains
② Great Plains-Rocky Mountain route
③ Mackenzie Valley-Great Lakes-
Mississippi Valley route—most
heavily traveled route
④ Atlantic coast route (bobolinks' favorite)
⑤ Atlantic Ocean route (plovers' favorite)
— SUMMER HOMES—northern limit

BIRDS' TRAVEL ROUTES

The turkey vulture soars in wide circles for hours at a time, looking for dead animals to feed upon. Though found over much of the United States, it prefers the South.

The red-tailed hawk, found over most of North America, also loves open spaces in which to soar. It looks for mice—not chickens, as many farmers think.

The crow is a bird of American and Canadian fields and woods. It is a clever, noisy, thieving rascal that likes to steal and hide bright things.

The nighthawk comes out on summer evenings all over North America. It dives and whirls over cities and farms and villages, catching insects.

The ruby-throated hummingbird is one of the smallest birds in the world. It is found only in eastern North America.

The goldfinch, often called a "wild canary," darts about the lawns and gardens of North America in flocks—except during nesting season.

The starling, brought from Europe, is now one of our most familiar city birds. It sings and squeaks from a favorite perch.

The cardinal is usually a year-round resident all over the United States. It is easy to see, and its loud whistle is easy to hear.

A few English sparrows were brought to America from England in 1850. Now they are everywhere—in city and country alike.

Scientists think birds have a migrating instinct which tells them just the right time to leave and return, and how to fly in the right direction on their trips.

Birds' feathers must be in perfect condition for their long flying trip. The young birds molt their first flying feathers, and grow their first grown-up ones. Old birds get rid of their worn-out feathers and grow new ones.

A bird's fuel for flying is stored in the layer of fat under its skin. Before leaving, birds spend a great deal of time eating and growing fat. Some birds stop and eat on their trips, but others have to fly many miles over the sea and can't stop for meals.

Old and young birds gather together in flocks before they start. They get in trim for their long journeys by making short trips back and forth from their feeding grounds in the daytime to their roosts at night. Perhaps you have seen swallows in July or August, resting in flocks on telephone wires during these first practice flights.

Each bird leaves for its winter or summer home at almost exactly the same time each year. Storms on the way may delay them, or good weather may speed them up, but, if the weather is much the same year after year, birds are likely to reach either their winter or summer homes on the very same day each year. The diagram on page 53 will show you how far some of our birds go in winter.

Some birds travel only by day. Day flyers include many birds that gather at night to roost. Among them are robins, crows, swallows, swifts, and bigger birds like hawks.

Many more birds travel by night than by day, and they find their way just as surely as those who fly in the daytime. Night fliers are shy, timid birds, like warblers and sparrows and thrushes, that are used to the covering of bushes and trees. They wait to travel more safely in the cover of night.

The last birds to leave in the fall are usually the first to return in the spring. They make short migrations and spend less time traveling. In March, the early birds, robins and grackles and red-winged blackbirds, arrive in the North. By the middle of May, in the northern part of the United States, more birds are on their travels than at any other time of year. June brings only stragglers —a few late-comers.

greater bird of paradise
(Aru Islands and
New Guinea)

cock-of-the-rock
(South America)

ostrich
(Africa)
largest bird
in the world

BIRDS
AROUND
THE WORLD

golden pheasant
(China)

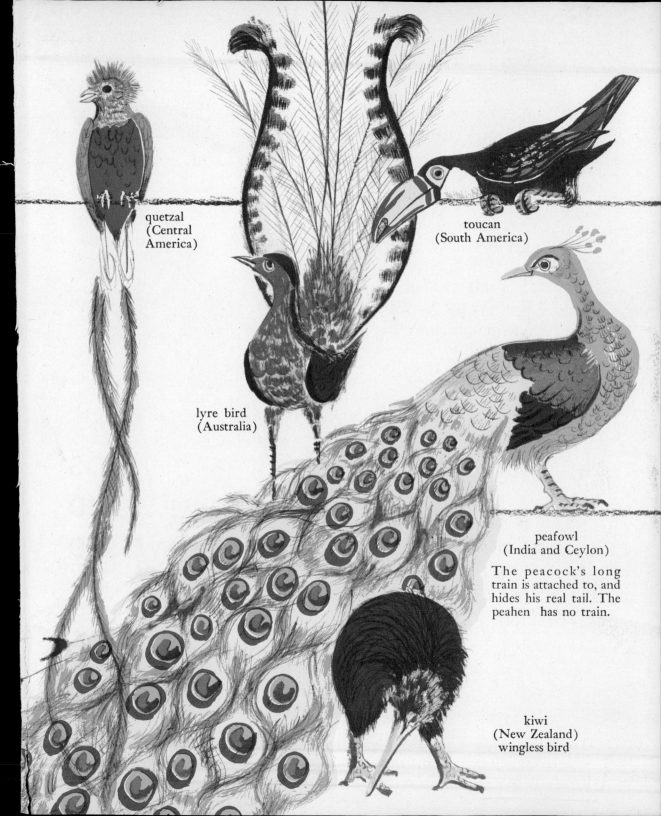

quetzal
(Central
America)

toucan
(South America)

lyre bird
(Australia)

peafowl
(India and Ceylon)

The peacock's long
train is attached to, and
hides his real tail. The
peahen has no train.

kiwi
(New Zealand)
wingless bird

Not all birds travel safely back and forth. No matter how strong birds' wings may be, how well they may be prepared for their trip, or how great their migrating instinct is, many run into storms and die at sea or are beaten down to earth. Some of them are gobbled up by bigger birds. Many fly against lighthouses and are killed. Others, flying across cities at night, bump into tall buildings, or wires.

KNOWING BIRDS

Everywhere you go you will see and hear birds. But to really make friends with them and know them by name you must stop and listen and watch. Then you can see for yourself the things they do and the way they live.

And you will see how valuable they are to us. The insect eaters help us get rid of the pests that harm our plants and trees. Owls and hawks catch small animals like mice and rats, that are troublesome to farmers. Birds that eat fruits and berries spread seeds in getting rid of their waste material. And by watching birds fly and glide and soar, and by studying how they are built, aviation experts have learned many things about airplane building.

The best time to go looking for birds is in the early morning, at daybreak. Then birds are busiest, and easiest to see. Try to take trips regularly all year through, so that you will be sure to see the birds migrating north in the spring, building their nests and feeding

60

their young in summer, and flying south in the fall.

By noticing, you will soon find the best spots to see birds. Swampy woodlands, places with low scrubby bushes, and edges of brooks are favorite places for birds. But seashores, edges of forests, fields, and even city parks and your own back garden will have their own special birds.

If you move quickly, birds will be frightened, so sometimes it is best to sit as quietly as a tree stump and let birds come to you. Then they will keep on doing things as naturally as if you weren't there. Whenever you do move, go slowly, and don't stand out in the open where they can see you.

One of the best ways to learn about birds is by going on trips with other bird watchers. If you don't know any, then join a bird club in your neighborhood or start one yourself. The National Audubon Society has Junior Audubon Clubs connected to local nature museums, schools, boy and girl scout troops and camps throughout the United States and Canada. If you write to the National Audubon Society, 1000 Fifth Avenue, New York 28, N. Y., or the Audubon Society of Canada, 177 Jarvis Street, Toronto 2, Canada, they will tell you what bird clubs are in your neighborhood, or how to go about starting a Junior Audubon Club yourself.

B I R D
P E T S

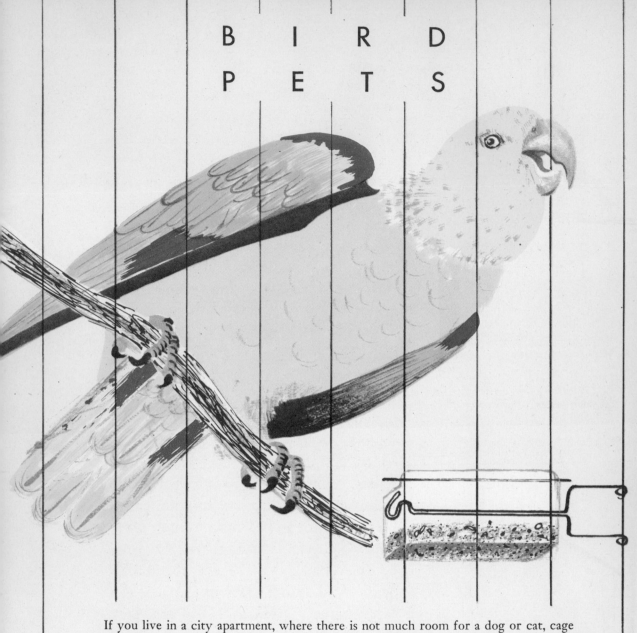

If you live in a city apartment, where there is not much room for a dog or cat, cage birds will make good pets. If you look after them well they will become quite tame. Canaries will sing for you, and parrots, parakeets and lovebirds can be trained to talk. If you keep a male and female together, you may even be able to raise baby birds.

POLLY is a Mexican yellow-head parrot. Yellow-head parrots make the best talkers among birds. They can be taught to say whole sentences, to sing songs, and to whistle tunes. Sometimes they are said to live to be over one hundred years old.

"Bongo" and his mate

"Richard"

BONGO and his mate are African lovebirds. When they play they nibble and scratch one another's heads.

RICHARD is a roller canary. Roller canaries make the best singers though other kinds of canaries may be prettier.

NICKEY is an Australian shell parakeet. In Australia he is called a budgereegar. He can say in a high voice, "What have you been doing?" "Merry Christmas, everybody," and lots of other things. Parakeets come in many different colors.

"Nickey"

 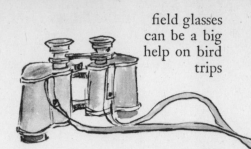

field glasses can be a big help on bird trips

In watching birds, a guidebook is a big help. Two good inexpensive ones that will fit into your pocket are *Birds*, by Zim and Gabrielson, and *How To Know The Birds*, by R. T. Peterson. You can get either of these at any large bookshop.

Take along a notebook and pencil for making notes and sketches of the birds you see. Jot down when and where you see them, what they are doing, and what their nests and eggs are like. If you keep your notebook from year to year it is fun to check on when you saw your first robin the year before, and to compare notes with other bird watchers.

BIRDS AND YOU

Birds need a quiet place to make a nest and raise a family. They need shady trees and bushy shrubs for protection from sun and storms and enemies, lots of food and water, and a spot to roost and spend the night. If you give them the things they need, you can have them nesting and wintering and even stopping over on their migration flights right in your backyard.

Birdhouses you can build yourself will also bring birds to nest in your garden. Not all birds like the same kinds of houses. If you are going to make some birdhouses which birds will want to live in, you might write to the Government Printing Office, Washington 25, D. C., and ask them to send you their Conservation Bulletin No. 14, called *Homes for Birds and How to Build Them*. It costs only ten cents, and it will tell you all you need to know.

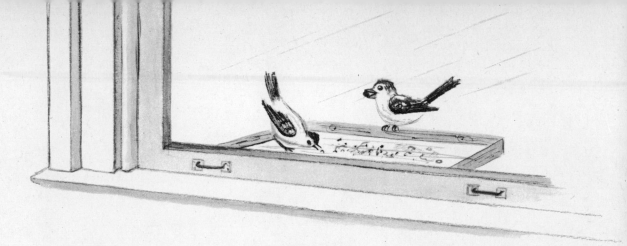

In wintertime, especially if you live where it is cold and there is snow on the ground, you can bring winter birds close to you by keeping a feeding tray outside your window sill in a protected place. Just a plain wooden shelf at least a foot square, with a little ledge all about to keep the food from blowing off, will do nicely.

Seed-eating birds, like juncos and grosbeaks, will eat oatmeal, sunflower seeds, cracked wheat and bread crumbs. For the insect eaters, you can make a suet-holder of wood or raffia or coarsely woven cloth, and tack it to a tree or a window ledge and fill it with beef suet, raw meat scraps, peanut butter or doughnut crumbs. This kind of food will bring woodpeckers, chickadees, nuthatches, creepers and jays to your window sill. Once you start, it is only fair of you to set food out every day, for birds get used to finding their meals on your shelf. Put fine gravel and a dish of water on the shelf, too.

suet holder
on tree

There is no end to the fun you can have with birds, and only a bird watcher will ever know the thrill of discovering a rare bird for the first time, or the wonder of watching a baby chick picking its way out of its shell, or the satisfaction of finding a pair of birds nesting in his very own nesting box, or the happy surprise of meeting old bird friends in a strange new country.

suet stick—
suet stuffed in holes
bored in branch of
soft wood

BIRDHOUSES
and the birds that will live in them

→ screech owl

← robin

bluebird →

purple martins

wren

flicker

DO YOU KNOW THAT . . .

All the starlings in North America are the offspring of only one hundred birds brought from Western Europe and released in Central Park, New York City, in 1890 and '91.

Ostriches do not hide their heads in sand when they are afraid, as most people think, but run stupidly in circles.

Before the days of penholders and nibs, people used a goose quill dipped in ink to write letters.

In China and Japan, cormorants are trained to fish. Tight collars about their necks keep them from swallowing their catch. Instead they are forced to drop their fish into a boat and return to the water for more.

Some plovers and egrets in Africa find their meals inside crocodiles' mouths. They eat the flies that buzz about inside or the scraps of food they find there.

After many days at sea, Columbus and his discouraged men saw birds flying about their ship. They knew then that land could not be far away, so they sailed on—and discovered America.

Primitive people have always used birds in their designs.

INDEX

(Numbers for full pages of pictures are in bold face type)